Gus Gets a Shell

By Sally Cowan

Gus the gull sat on the shed with Dad.

Shan's ship had come in.

It had lots of clams in shells.

"Dad," said Gus.

"Can I get a shell?"

But Gus did not get a shell.

He can smell hot chips!

Some kids tossed chips
to the big gulls.

Gus ran to scoff a chip.

"Get off!" yelled a big gull.
"**My** chip! **My** chip!"

Gus sat at the chip shop.

He sat and sat till
the big gulls went.

But the kids went, too,
and the chip shop shut.

Gus got a clam shell.

But its lid was shut!

Gus got the shell and went up ... up ... up!

Gus tossed the shell.

It fell on the shed with a thud!

"Yum, yum!" said Gus.
"I like clams in shells!"

CHECKING FOR MEANING

1. Why did Gus sit at the chip shop? *(Literal)*

2. Why did Gus go up and up with the clam shell? *(Literal)*

3. Why do you think Dad was on the shed with Gus? *(Inferential)*

EXTENDING VOCABULARY

shell	What sound does the digraph *sh–* make in this word? If you took away the digraph *sh–*, what other letter or letters could you put at the start to make a new word?
chip	What does the word *chip* mean in this story? What else can *chip* mean? If you were to *chip* a plate, or *chip* your tooth, what would that mean?
shut	What does the word *shut* mean? What is another word that has a similar meaning? Replace the word *shut* in a sentence with this new word. Does it change the meaning of the sentence?

MOVING BEYOND THE TEXT

1. How do young birds learn how to find food?

2. What other skills do baby birds need to learn to be able to survive?

3. If you had some clams in shells, how would you open them? Why?

4. What food do we usually eat with chips? What other foods do we often eat together? E.g. bacon and eggs.

SPEED SOUNDS

sh	ch	th	th	wh	qu	ph

voiced   unvoiced

PRACTICE WORDS

Shan's

shed

ship

chips

shells

shop

shut

thud

shell

chip